愛迪生

Heroes and Role Models | Non-Fiction Series

Copyright © 2022 by Level Learning, INC. and Washington Yu Ying PCS™
Original and Edited Text Copyright © 2022 by Washington Yu Ying PCS™

All rights reserved. No part of this book in whole or part may be reproduced without written permission from the publisher.

Published by Level Learning, INC.

Content Contributors:
Washington Yu Ying PCS™
Level Learning - Ya-Ching Chang

Illustrations by: Josh Taira

Leveling classification based on Level Learning standard. For full description, visit www.levellearning.com

ISBN 978-1-64040-035-1
Traditional Chinese Edition

About Level Learning:

Level Learning provides a literacy focused curriculum specifically designed for K-12 Chinese as a Second Language classrooms. Our program offers 20 levels of specific and detailed objectives, leveled texts and passages, mastery-based online assessment, and analytics to enable data-driven instruction. Level Learning reading curriculum for both literature and informational text emphasize grammar and comprehension skills to help teachers develop confident and independent Chinese language readers. The non-fiction series of books are specifically designed to support our informational text course based on multiple national standards. To learn more about our entire offering, visit www.levellearning.com.

About Washington Yu Ying PCS™:

Washington Yu Ying PCS is a Mandarin English dual language immersion International Baccalaureate (IB) World school. Yu Ying's mission is to inspire and prepare young people to create a better world by challenging them to reach their full potential in a nurturing Chinese/English educational environment. Yu Ying's comprehensive IB, dual immersion curriculum equips students with global competencies for success in the real world. As a leader in immersion education, Yu Ying is determined to advance Chinese language programs and global citizenry education by helping other schools create and strengthen their Chinese programs. For more information, email: products@washingtonyuying.org

愛迪生是美國著名的發明家，出生於1847年。他從小就有非常強的好奇心，常常問一些奇怪的問題，有時候大人們都不知道這些問題的答案。

因為愛迪生喜歡在學校不停地問問題，這讓老師很頭疼，所以他只上了十二個星期的小學，就留在家裡一邊和媽媽學習一邊做實驗。在這段時間裡，愛迪生不僅學習了大量的知識，而且也有了更多時間做他感興趣的科學實驗。

做實驗需要買大量的材料，而且有些材料也不便宜。對於一個小孩子來說，這毫無疑問是一件困難的事情。為了有足夠的錢做實驗，在十二歲的時候，愛迪生開始在火車上賣糖果和報紙。他把這些錢都存下來，用於做實驗。

就這樣，愛迪生在各種科學實驗中長大了。長大後的愛迪生更加明確了自己的目標。他蓋了一間實驗室，和他的同事在裡面發明了很多東西。電燈就是其中一個發明。

在發明電燈以後,愛迪生又發明了一個電力系統,讓電燈泡可以發光。那時的他還不知道,就是這個小小的電燈泡,對全世界的人們都有著非常重要的意義。

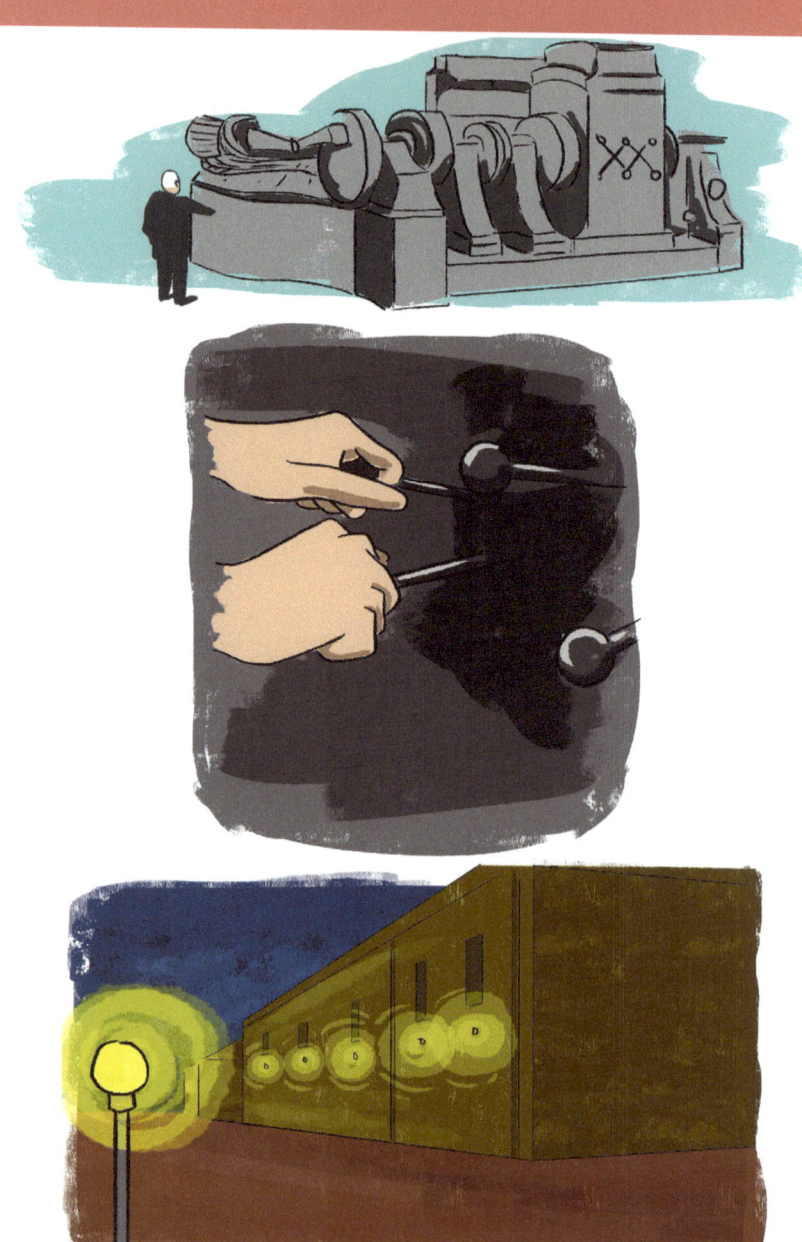

1882年的一天，愛迪生打開了一個開關，給紐約的85間房子帶來光亮。這是人類歷史上第一次使用電燈照明。從此以後，夜晚也因為這些光亮變得更加美麗。

除了電燈以外，愛迪生還有一千多項發明。愛迪生的發明，改變了我們的世界，也改善了我們的生活。

Glossary

	Pinyin	English Definition
著名	zhù míng	famous
發明家	fā míng jiā	inventor
好奇心	hào qí xīn	curious
頭疼	tóu téng	headache
大量	dà liàng	a lot of
知識	zhī shi	knowledge
感興趣	gǎn xìng qù	interested
科學實驗	kē xué shí yàn	science experiment
材料	cái liào	material
便宜	pián yi	cheap
毫無疑問	háo wú yí wèn	no doubt
足夠	zú gòu	enough
存	cún	to save
目標	mù biāo	goal
實驗室	shí yàn shì	laboratory

	Pinyin	English Definition
電力系統	diàn lì xì tǒng	power systems
意義	yì yì	meaning, consequence
開關	kāi guān	generator
照明	zhào míng	light, illumination
改變	gǎi biàn	to change
改善	gǎi shàn	to improve

www.ingramcontent.com/pod-product-compliance
Lightning Source LLC
Chambersburg PA
CBHW041226070526
44584CB00001B/109